4/05

PLAZA

W9-BFE-683

Art and
Architecture

Stewart Ross

LUCENT
BOOKS ®

THOMSON
GALE

San Diego • Detroit • New York • San Francisco • Cleveland • New Haven, Conn. • Waterville, Maine • London • Munich

Originally published by Hodder Wayland,
an imprint of Hodder Children's Books,
a division of Hodder Headline Limited
338 Euston Road, London NW1 3BH

For more information, contact
Lucent Books
27500 Drake Rd.
Farmington Hills, MI 48331-3535
Or you can visit our Internet site at http://www.gale.com

Design: Peta Morey
Commissioning Editor: Jane Tyler
Editor: Liz Gogerly
Picture Researcher: Glass Onion Pictures
Consultant: Malcolm Barber

We are grateful to the following for permission to reproduce photographs:
Art Archive Limited 4, 6, 7, 9, 10, 13, 14, 15, 18, 19, 21, 22, 23, 24, 25 (bottom), 26, 27 (bottom), 29, 31, 32, 33, 38, 40, 44, 45; AKG Images 8, 11, 17, 25 (top); Bridgeman Art Library 5/ San Francesco, Upper Church, Assisi, Italy 12/ Duomo, Florence, Italy 16/Mezquita, Cordoba, Spain 20/ Westminster Abbey, London, UK 27 (top)/ Fontenay Abbey, Montbard, Burgundy, France 30; British Museum (title) 42 (top and bottom); Crown Copyright reproduced courtesy of Historic Scotland 39; National Trust 37, 43; Reading Museum 34; Topham Picturepoint 28, 35, 36, 41

Cover picture: © Archivo Iconographico, S.A./CORBIS

Please note: Dates after monarchs refer to dates of reign unless otherwise noted. Words in **bold** can be found in the glossary.

LIBRARY OF CONGRESS CATALOGING-IN-PUBLICATION DATA

Ross, Stewart,
   Art and Architecture / by Stewart Ross.
     p. cm. — (Medieval realms)
   Includes bibliographical references and index.
    ISBN 1-59018-534-X (alk. paper)

Printed in China

Contents

Romanesque Architecture

IN ABOUT 1000 A.D. a new movement in European art and architecture was born. Known as Romanesque, it was a lively blend of the style of ancient Rome with the more recent ideas and designs of Germany, France, and **Byzantium** (the city of Istanbul and its surrounding region). It lasted for about 150 years before developing into the Gothic style (see pages 10–17).

Romanesque architecture grew out of a burst of Christian enthusiasm that began in the tenth century. This created a need for more and larger stone-built monasteries and churches. To increase the space within them, builders constructed roofs

Among the finest examples of Romanesque architecture are the roofs on the church of St. Foy, Conques, France.

Romanesque Decoration

In northern Europe Romanesque decoration tended to be fairly straightforward. The arch above a doorway, for example, might be carved with a zigzag pattern. Stone columns were sometimes cut with spiral or chain-mail designs. Although simple, in their day these patterns looked much more striking than they do today because they were painted with bright colors, such as red, orange, and yellow.

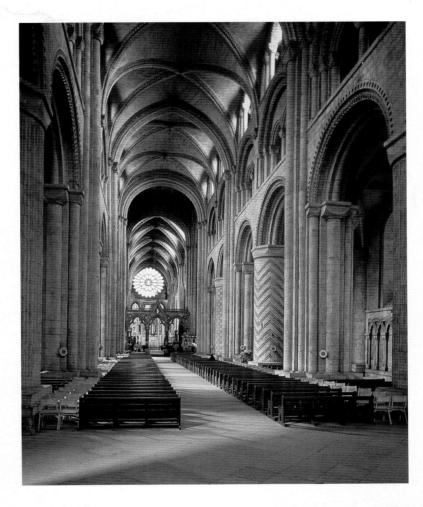

The sturdy Romanesque pillars along the nave of Durham Cathedral, England, show the confidence and skill of their Norman builders.

(**vaults**) of rounded stone arches. This is called barrel vaulting because it resembles the shape of an upturned barrel cut in half.

Barrel vaults were extremely heavy, so pillars and walls had to be very thick to carry them. Windows and doors (also rounded like the vaults) were kept small so as not to weaken the walls. This made the insides of most Romanesque churches and cathedrals impressive but dark and somber.

Austere Beauty

Several different forms of Romanesque architecture emerged. The most advanced was in France, producing such stark but lovely buildings as the **abbey** church of St. Foy (St. Faith) in Conques. Its carvings are among the wonders of the early medieval world. Similarly glorious Romanesque carving can be seen on the **tympanum** of Ribe Cathedral, Denmark, which shows Christ's body being brought down from the cross.

With the exception of Edward the Confessor's abbey at Westminster, Romanesque architecture came to Britain with the Normans' conquest of 1066. In eagerness to bring England into line with the rest of Europe, most **Anglo-Saxon** buildings (see panel) were pulled down and replaced by massive new Norman ones.

All but one English Romanesque cathedral were built as part of monasteries. Many were rebuilt in the later **Middle Ages**, although plenty of Norman architecture remains. Well-known English examples are the cathedrals of Canterbury and Durham.

Saxon Architecture

The English building style before 1066 is known as Anglo-Saxon, from the German tribes (Angles and Saxons) who settled the country 600 years earlier. The only Anglo-Saxon buildings to survive are stone churches. They are small, normally with rounded arches over the doors and windows. Several features, like carved decoration, are clearly influenced by European work.

Romanesque Art: Painting

NEARLY ALL early medieval painting was religious. That is to say, its aim was to reinforce the viewer's faith and, perhaps, explain Christian teaching to them. It consisted of wall paintings (murals and frescoes) inside churches and monasteries, painted panels, tapestries, and book decoration. Tapestries, and the decoration of books, known as **illumination**, are discussed on pages 8–9 and 32–33.

This charming thousand-year-old fresco of the life of St. Alexis, popularly known as the "Man of God," adorns the ancient church of San Clemente, Rome.

Wall Painting

There were two techniques of wall painting. The tempera method involved painting dry plaster with a mix of paint and egg yolk, which fixed the paint to the surface. The fresco technique, pioneered in Italy, involved painting while the plaster was still wet. This required great skill: the artist had to finish before the plaster dried, and there was no chance of correcting a mistake. As a result, fresco paintings were very bold and lively.

Sadly, very little early medieval wall painting has survived. As far as we can tell, much of it was simply pattern and design. Where the work showed people, the style was heavily influenced by Byzantium (as with Romanesque architecture, see pages 4–5). The artist was more concerned with the religious message than with being realistic.

An example is the eleventh-century fresco of the life of St. Alexis, visible in San Clemente, Rome (see page 6). The picture is not intended to be lifelike. Instead, its images are symbols of the popular saint and his godly deeds. According to legend, Alexis gave up worldly wealth and lived as an unknown servant in the house of his rich father, sleeping under the stairs.

Different countries developed painting styles of their own. Spanish wall painting, for instance, was rather stiff and formal. Italy, because it was closer to Byzantium, was more influenced by the art of that city.

The French Romanesque style is best preserved in two famous sets of murals. The abbey church of Saint-Savin-sur-Gartempe contains beautiful murals illustrating well-known Christian stories. The picture above, for example, shows St. Cyprian and St. Savinus before the Roman official Galerius Maximus who ordered their execution for heresy in 258 B.C.

Distinguished by their halos, St. Savinus and St. Cyprian stand before the Roman official Galerius Maximus in this twelfth-century fresco found inside the abbey church of Saint-Savin-sur-Gartempe, France.

Abbot Desiderius decorates his new eleventh-century church at Monte Cassino:

After having installed the ceiling below the timber work, he decorated it admirably with various colours and designs. He also had the walls painted a beautiful variety of colours.... He ordered the remaining three wings of the atrium [entrance] painted outside and inside with various scenes from the Old and New Testament, and all the wings paved with marble.

The Chronicle of Monte Cassino (text simplified by the author)

Romanesque Art: Tapestry

A TAPESTRY is a fabric painstakingly and skillfully woven to produce an **abstract** image or a picture. The weaver bases his work on a design, known as a cartoon, created by an artist. Medieval tapestries were nearly all woven from wool, with silk threads sometimes added for brightness.

Very few tapestries survive from the Romanesque period. Perhaps the oldest is that made for the church of St. Gereon, Cologne, Germany. Later, the European tapestry industry was centered in Arras in Flanders—between 1423 and 1467 the city housed fifty-nine tapestry workshops. By this time the subjects were no longer just religious. Philip the Good, Duke of Burgundy (1419–1467), for example, ordered a set of tapestries showing the life of Alexander the Great (see below).

One of the magnificent mid-fifteenth-century tapestries made in Tournai, Belgium, tells the story of Alexander the Great. Note how its creators placed the scene in an entirely medieval setting. The tapestry now hangs in the Galleria Doria-Pamphili, Rome.

The Bayeux Tapestry

The famous Bayeux Tapestry is in fact not a tapestry but an embroidery. It was probably stitched in Canterbury, England, to adorn the cathedral of Bishop Odo of Bayeux, France, who was the brother of England's William the Conqueror (1066–1087). Measuring 230 feet long and 20 inches wide, today it is on display in Bayeux, Normandy, France.

The Tapestry, one of the most valuable pieces of early medieval art in existence, consists of over seventy scenes. These are stitched with eight colors of wool onto a linen background. The simple but charming design and the lively, sometimes funny, decorations make viewing it, even a thousand years since its creation, a truly memorable experience.

Telling the story of the fight for the throne of England in 1066, the Tapestry is also an invaluable source of historical evidence. It offers information on a wide range of matters, from everyday dress to weapons, and William's claim to the throne. However, it is unclear on one of British history's famous mysteries—was King Harold (1066) really killed by an arrow in the eye?

Thousand Flowers

The late Gothic period produced a charming series of tapestries known as *mille-fleurs* (thousand flowers). These lively scenes of late-medieval life were produced in Brussels, Bruges (both in present-day Belgium), and the Loire Valley (France). A dark background, covered with flowers, plants, and creatures, is the setting for some imaginary scene, such as "The Hunt of the Unicorn" (now hanging in the Metropolitan Museum of Art, New York).

Duke William (later William the Conqueror) receives a messenger—a scene from the eleventh-century embroidery, the Bayeux Tapestry.

The Gothic Revolution: Architecture

A REVOLUTION in European architecture and art began in the first half of the twelfth century. It started in and around Paris, France, and eventually spread across most of the **Continent**. Since the sixteenth century the new style has been known as Gothic, after the tribes of Goths that invaded the Roman empire in the fourth and fifth centuries. It broke away from the **Classical** style of ancient Greece and Rome.

Builders brilliantly overcame the problem of the weight of Romanesque vaults (see page 5). One of the best-known examples of the new design is the **choir** of Abbot Suger's great cathedral of St. Denis, just north of Paris. It was rebuilt between 1136 and 1147 to show off its holy **relics** and attract **pilgrims**.

The soaring nave of the twelfth-century St. Denis Cathedral, France, is a fine early example of the Gothic style.

Abbot Suger describes his work at St. Denis, making it clear that he could have done nothing without God's help:

Since in the front part, toward the north, at the main entrance with the main doors, the narrow hall was squeezed in on either side by twin towers neither high nor very sturdy but threatening ruin, we began, with the help of God, strenuously to work on this part, having laid very strong material foundations for a straight nave and twin towers, and most strong spiritual ones.

Teresa G. Frisch, *Gothic Art 1140–c. 1450: Sources and Documents*

The enormous nave of Lincoln Cathedral, England, was completed in 1233. The pointed arches direct the eyes of the worshippers toward heaven.

Four features marked Gothic architecture. First, builders carried the weight of the roof on delicate stone bars, known as ribs, filling the space between with light panels. Second, rounded arches were replaced with more flexible pointed ones. Third, the weight of the vault was carried down the ribs. These took the weight onto piers (or pillars) instead of to the walls.

Pointing to Heaven

The fourth development was the use of **buttresses** (see page 15) to carry the downward and outward weight of the roof away from the walls. Now that the walls no longer carried great weight, they could be much taller and pierced with larger and more delicate windows. These were divided up by fine stone bars known as **tracery**.

Many cathedrals, such as Notre-Dame de Paris, were soon being rebuilt in the elegant and lofty new style. In England the Early Gothic style is known as Early English. Its typical features are churches of great length, such as Lincoln Cathedral, shown above, and tall pointed windows, known as **lancets**.

Another delightful Early Gothic feature is the marble pillar that looks as if it is made up of a cluster of smaller shafts. With soaring spires pointing the faithful to heaven, Gothic architecture mirrored the deeply religious medieval mind.

Bells

Church bells, marking the passing of the day and calling people to prayer, played a key role in medieval life. Bells were originally made by monks. By the eleventh century skilled bell makers (founders) were traveling around Europe casting bigger and bigger bells from molten bronze. They were hung in church and cathedral bell towers, some of which (the famous Leaning Tower of Pisa, for example) were detached from the church itself.

The Gothic Revolution: Art

BY THE early thirteenth century European painting, like architecture, was changing from the Romanesque to the Gothic style. Its main features were a new softness (except in Germany) and, most important of all, greater **realism**. This came about because art was reflecting changes in religion and society rather than somehow getting better. The popularity of the Virgin Mary (mother of Christ), for example, led to artists trying to show her in a more realistic human form. As the influence of Byzantium fell away, Italian artists developed styles and techniques of their own that would gradually spread across the rest of the Continent.

Two technical advances pioneered in Italy helped to produce the new realism. One was the discovery of light—the realization that the way light falls on a subject is as important as the subject itself. The second was a gradual understanding of the **laws of perspective**. This enabled near and distant objects to be shown realistically in relation to each other.

Paintings such as this of St. Francis show the advance made by the Italian painter Giotto di Bondone in understanding how light falls on a subject. It is instructive to compare it, for example, with the figures on page 6.

Portraits

One of the most striking ways to see how medieval art developed is through portraits. In the early Middle Ages artists made little or no effort to represent a human likeness in their pictures. This began to change in the late thirteenth century, and by the fifteenth century, for the first time, we have accurate likenesses of a whole range of men and women.

The Italian artist Giotto (*c.* 1266–1337) made the most startling advances in Gothic painting. His frescoes at Assisi, showing the life of St. Francis, are one of the treasures of Western art. Equally interesting are the huge and realistic landscape frescoes painted in Siena by Ambrogio Lorenzetti (*c.* 1280–1348). Byzantine influence is entirely replaced by that of ancient Rome, a significant step toward the future.

The Last Judgement

Paintings were an important way of delivering religious messages to **congregations** who could not read. The Last Judgement was one of the most popular and powerful scenes depicted on the inside walls of medieval churches. On Judgement Day—also known as Doomsday—it was believed that Jesus Christ would return to Earth to judge the living and the dead. Those who had lived without sin would go to join the saints in heaven; sinners would be cast into the eternal torment of hell.

The Last Judgement pictured inside the vast castlelike brick cathedral of Sainte-Cécile in Albi, France, built between 1277 and 1515, is particularly impressive. The painting, which reaches almost from the floor to the towering roof, shows the special punishments in hell for each type of sinner. Early punishment is shown with horrible realism. We see the greedy, for example, continually forced to eat and drink more than they can hold.

The fourteenth-century Italian painter Cennino describes how to paint a face in his handbook for artists:

I will give you the exact proportions of a man…. First … the face is divided into three parts, namely, the forehead, one; the nose, another; and from the nose to the chin, another. From the side of the nose through the whole length of the eye, [is] one of these measures.

Teresa G. Frisch, *Gothic Art 1140–c. 1450: Sources and Documents*.

By the fourteenth century art was no longer exclusively religious. This painting, for example, shows good government represented by Magnanimity, Temperance, and Justice.

Gothic Glory

THE GOTHIC STYLE of building was always developing. By about 1225, for instance, Early Gothic was becoming more complicated, gradually changing toward the High Gothic. On the continent of Europe this is known as the *Rayonnant* (meaning radiant) style. In England, where it did not appear until nearly a century later, it is called Decorated.

As the English name suggests, the new emphasis was on decoration as much as overall shape and form. More delicate vaults were built, with ribs that spread like the veins in a leaf. Windows were larger, with more glass and complicated tracery. Carvings of foliage, animals, saints, and beasts appeared wherever there was a suitable niche, knob, or joint. Nevertheless, as with earlier religious architecture, the purpose was still the same: to glorify God by honoring him with the most magnificent works people could produce.

The choir of Laon Cathedral, France, illuminated by a glorious circular stained glass window (1227), is an example of Gothic architecture at its most radiant.

The construction of a great cathedral was a vastly expensive enterprise to which many hundreds of people contributed. Here a benefactor of Chartres is remembered:

Likewise [on this day there died] Robert of Blevia, procurator [administrator] of this holy church, a man kind and tenderly compassionate toward the poor, who adorned this church with a silk cope [hood], a dalmatic [robe] and tunic.... In addition, he donated ... £25.00 for the construction of one pillar.

Robert Branner, *Chartres Cathedral*

This picture clearly shows the carved buttresses supporting the roof at the eastern end of Notre-Dame Cathedral, Reims, France.

Chartres Cathedral

The splendid early-thirteenth-century cathedral at Chartres in France is a fine example of the developing *Rayonnant* style. The weight of the roof is carried down elegant pillars capped with carvings of leaves. The **boss** stones, where the roof ribs (see page 11) meet at their highest point, are similarly carved with leaves and creatures.

Outside, the building is supported by traditional-style buttresses. On top of these, two levels of flying buttresses (see panel right) stretch across the roofs of the **aisles**. They are decorated with columns and niches for statues of saints. At the west end of the building is what would become the hallmark of the *Rayonnant* style—a great round rose window filled with rich-colored glass.

Buttresses

A simple buttress is a prop against a wall to stop it from toppling over. When a roof other than a flat one is placed on top of a wall, the pressure is both downward and outward. Buttresses help bear this pressure. If they are solid, however, they cut down the light entering the building. Medieval builders solved this problem with the flying buttress. This did away with the part of the buttress nearest the wall, so it flew outward directly from the roof to the foundations.

High Gothic Architecture

HIGH (OR LATE) Gothic architecture developed in different ways across Europe. Generally, though, on mainland Europe the *Rayonnant* style was followed by the even more ornate Flamboyant (spectacular or showing-off) style, while the English reverted to the cleaner Perpendicular (see panel below). These styles endured until the early sixteenth century, when the Gothic was going out of fashion. Even so, it lingered on in some places for another eighty or so years.

The cathedral of Santa Maria del Fiore stands proudly above the other buildings in the skyline of the city of Florence, Italy. The cathedral, planned in the late thirteenth century, was built over six centuries. Its most famous feature, the magnificent dome, was built between 1420 and 1434.

English Perpendicular

In the late Middle Ages, as European church architecture became more highly decorated, in England it became more restrained. Key features of this Perpendicular style were precise workmanship in stone, creating even larger windows, flatter arches and delightful vaults in the shape of a half-cone or fan. These can be seen at their best in the superb chapel attached to King's College, Cambridge, built at the end of the fifteenth century.

Italy never really adopted the Gothic style of northern Europe. There are some magnificent Gothic buildings—Milan's white marble cathedral for example—but this is an exception. In most parts of the country the influence of the ancient Romans was never fully erased. In the early fifteenth century it took a new and remarkable form in the huge dome that tops Santa Maria del Fiore Cathedral in Florence. Beneath it, the rest of the cathedral is essentially Gothic.

Width and Variety

In contrast, Spanish architecture was influenced by the Muslims who governed the southern part of the peninsula until the end of the fifteenth century (see pages 18–19). While French Gothic emphasized a building's height and the English its length, the Spanish tended to go for width. The broad spaces of Gerona Cathedral illustrate this well.

Elsewhere, builders, priests, and ordinary men and women expressed their faith in a rich variety of beautiful buildings. Flying buttresses (see page 15) reached their most dramatic on Prague Cathedral, in the present-day Czech Republic (see right). In the German city of Munich, a completely different-looking church appeared. This was the fifteenth-century *Frauenkirche*, built of brick with rows of simple windows and extraordinary spiral pillars. The twin fourteenth-century towers of the cathedral at Roskilde, Denmark, offer another interesting example of brick construction.

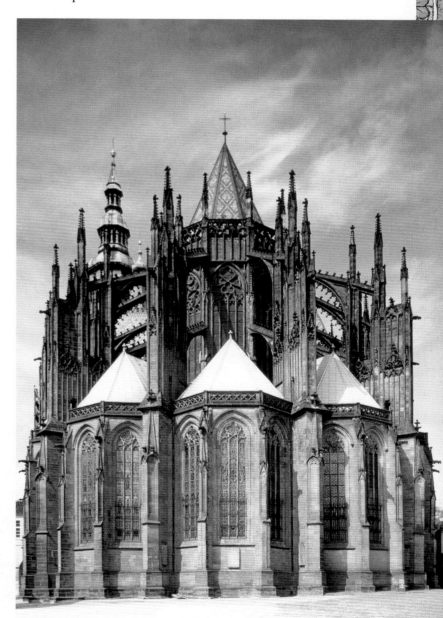

The picture shows the cathedral of St. Vitus in Prague, the capital of the Czech Republic.

Moorish Architecture

THE OCCUPATION of Spanish territory by Muslim Moors between the eighth and fifteenth centuries introduced there a wholly different style of architecture and art. Unique in Western Europe, it took its inspiration from the ancient civilizations of the Near East based on such great cities as Cairo, Baghdad, and Damascus.

The main differences between Moorish and Gothic architecture were the arrangement of religious buildings, the shape of arches, and the style of decoration. Moorish architects also liked using brick and stucco (plaster) while their Christian counterparts worked largely in stone.

The original Islamic design of the interior of the mosque-cathedral at Córdoba, Spain, was rearranged by Christian builders. But a wonderful forest of pillars remains.

Three Phases

Spanish-Moorish architecture went through three phases. The first, known as the Caliphate era (eighth to eleventh centuries), is remembered mainly for its construction of mosques, although palaces and fortresses were also built. All mosques followed the same basic pattern: a square prayer room with a small hollow facing Mecca, a courtyard containing a pool for washing, and a minaret (a tower from which the faithful are called to prayer). The most famous mosque from this period is that in Córdoba (see panel), whose roof is supported by an amazing 850 columns (see page 18).

The second, or Almohad, phase of Moorish architecture lasted from the twelfth to the thirteenth centuries. It used the same brick construction but the decoration (see pages 20–21) was much simpler. The traditional Moorish horseshoe arch now rose to a point at the top.

Nasrid architecture (fourteenth to fifteenth centuries) returned to the older, more elaborate form, although in a more sophisticated way. Refined decoration, especially around windows, lay at the heart of the style. Its most famous example is the Alhambra (Red Castle) in Granada. Of the many splendid halls, chambers, and courtyards, perhaps the most eye-catching, after the Court of Lions (see picture at right), is the Hall of the Ambassadors. A dome of cedarwood covers the ceiling, and the walls are adorned with ornate quotations from the Koran and inscriptions praising Moorish princes.

The delicacy and lightness of later Spanish Islamic architecture is evident in the fourteenth-century Court of Lions, part of the famous Alhambra palace in Granada, Spain.

Córdoba's Mosque-Cathedral

The first Muslims to arrive in Córdoba shared a church with Christians. This was later demolished to make way for the famous mosque. In the thirteenth century the Christians recaptured the city and converted part of the inside of the mosque into a cathedral. Then, in the sixteenth century, a second cathedral was built within the mosque, this time by cutting away the middle to erect traditional high vaults.

Islamic Art

THE PURPOSE of the bulk of Islamic and Christian art of the medieval period was the same: praising God and educating people about God. The way the two faiths went about this, however, was quite different. Christians did it with pictures, Muslims with words. This was because the Koran forbids representation of humans and animals in case people begin worshipping them rather than God.

As a consequence, Islamic art concentrated on decoration that did not show shapes of real things like people or animals. There were, for example, no pictures or carvings of the Prophet Muhammad or other holy figures. Instead, one of the most widely used forms of decoration was a text from the Muslims' holy book, the Koran.

This impressive decorated doorway leads to the Prayer Hall of the Great Mosque in Córdoba, Spain (see pages 18–19).

It became customary to take a short phrase such as Allah Al-Akbah! (God is Almighty) and write it out in extremely flamboyant and ornate handwriting. This would be difficult using the western European alphabet, but the Arabic alphabet, with its long, flowing letters, is ideally suited to such **calligraphic art**.

Lattices and Lozenges

Other forms of decoration included building in different-colored bricks, especially around the top of the familiar horseshoe-shaped arches. Foliation—taking the shape of a leaf—was a widely used decoration in plaster molding, brick, and paint. So too was latticework, created by cutting intricate patterns and shapes within a thin sheet of wood or metal. Much latticework and other decoration is described as geometric, meaning it took the form of common shapes found in geometry, such as circles, semicircles, and lozenges.

As well as buildings, Moorish craft workers embellished a range of smaller goods. These included tiles, weapons, chests, and brocade (silken cloth). They were decorated in a style similar to that of buildings with inscriptions, carving, enamel, and paint. It was from portable objects such as these, rather than from architecture, that Islamic art had some influence on western Europe. This happened not just from the interchange of goods in Spain, but also from the experiences of **crusaders**.

The uniformity of Islamic design is shown in the similarity between the architecture of Moorish Spain and that of Turkey, here represented by the interior of the mosque of Sultan Selim II at Edirne, Turkey.

Picture Windows

A MEDIEVAL CHURCH or cathedral without its stained glass is like a color film in black and white—much of the magic is lost. Sadly, war, storm, and fanaticism have destroyed all too many medieval stained glass windows. We are fortunate, though, that enough remain to show us what magical glory they once brought to the interiors of most religious buildings.

Stained glass windows were made from small panels of colored glass, illustrated with enamel paint and pieced together with strips of lead. The idea, which originated in medieval Europe, probably came from seeing **mosaics**.

The first leaded window dates from the ninth century, and the earliest complete picture window (in Augsburg, Germany)

Adding Color

Twelfth-century stained glass windows used only very limited colors. These varied according to the thickness of the glass. The five basic colors were obtained as follows:

For green a compound (oxide) of iron was added to clear glass.

For yellow **antimony** was added to clear glass.

For purple **manganese** was added to clear glass.

For blue **cobalt** was added to clear glass.

For ruby copper was added to clear glass.

The majestic rose window in the western façade of Reims Cathedral, France, symbolizes the beauty of holiness.

Medieval life frozen in colored glass: a detail from a late- thirteenth-century window in Canterbury Cathedral, England, depicts pilgrims on their way to worship at the shrine of the holy martyr, St. Thomas Becket.

from the twelfth century. Many regard such twelfth- and thirteenth-century windows, made with simple designs and a few very rich colors, to be the most beautiful of all.

Window making was an extremely skilled and painstaking task. Chartres Cathedral, for example, has 26,900 square feet of stained glass in 176 separate windows. These took nine master craftsmen, each working with several assistants, over forty years to complete.

Pictures and Stories

As with tapestry and wall painting, the object of pictures in stained glass was twofold. First, they were works of beauty in their own right, filling the inside of the building with glorious colors. Second, they were there to instruct the illiterate majority and remind them of Bible stories and teachings. In the earliest stained glass windows this was done with single, dramatic pictures. The most popular was Christ on the cross.

Later, as windows became larger, they told whole stories. The Ascension Window in Le Mans Cathedral, France, for example, depicts Jesus going up to heaven. Sometimes interesting local detail is added. The thirteenth-century Dean's Eye window in Lincoln Cathedral, for instance, is largely concerned with the Last Judgement (see page 13). However, it also shows the entry into the city of the body of St. Hugh, the bishop who set about rebuilding the cathedral after an earthquake.

The Bishop of Le Mans describes how the tradespeople who worked on the cathedral chose to be remembered:

[They] … made a window … [in] which they themselves are depicted [shown] in their trades. Nor did we think we should withhold praise of them, simply because they made a window in which they depicted themselves in their trades, for, after all, they did make a splendid window.

Teresa G. Frisch, *Gothic Art c. 1140–1450: Sources and Documents*

Sculpture: Decoration

RELIGIOUS BUILDINGS of the Romanesque and Early Gothic period (roughly 1000–1200) were charmingly decorated with carvings in stone. Early Romanesque carving was often very simple—just regular patterns around doors and windows and on top of pillars. By the twelfth century, when the glorious stone above the west door (the tympanum) of the church at Conques, France, was created, medieval sculpture had developed into a superb art form. The Conques tympanum, depicting God's Last Judgement of the world and all its peoples, contains 124 figures that were once brightly painted.

Botany in Stone

Romanesque sculpture is not meant to be realistic. It is about images and their message—Jesus Christ, for example, is always shown in a special posture and much bigger than other figures. Gothic sculpture, on the other hand, becomes more realistic. This applies to objects such as leaves as much as people. It is said that the carved foliage at Reims Cathedral, France, is like a botany lesson.

Gilbert Crispin, Abbot of Westminster (1085–1117), defends having images in his church as aids to worship:

In God's honour we make pictures, in God's honour we make carvings, in God's honour we also make graven [carved] images. But we do not adore them or worship them as if they were divine [holy].

Caecilia Davis-Weyer, *Early Medieval Art 300–1150*

The famous tympanum above the south entrance of St. Peter's Church, Moissac, France, shows God judging all people—living and dead—on the last day of the world.

The finest Early Gothic sculpture is usually to be found on the west façades of large churches and cathedrals. This part of the building is where the main door is and it has plenty of wall space suitable for decoration. Some of the most important examples are at St. Denis and Chartres in France. The most unusual English example dates from much later: The lively façade of Exeter Cathedral was finished in the mid–fourteenth century.

German Early Gothic work is also delightful. Some of the most interesting pieces are to be found in the west choir of Naumburg Cathedral. Here, high up in the **triforium**, stand statues of those who had given money to build the cathedral.

Those who funded the thirteenth-century building of Naumburg Cathedral, Germany, are preserved as statues in the triforium. From the details of their faces to the hang of their medieval clothes, they are relaxed and realistically human.

Misericords

Monks' seats in church were hinged so they folded back when the occupant stood up. To take the weight off their feet, a little ledge known as a **misericord** (mercy) was often attached to the bottom of the seat. The lower side of a misericord was often carved with amusing (and sometimes rude) images and scenes that could not normally be seen.

This fifteenth-century misericord, found in Roskilde Cathedral, Denmark, expresses the artist's emotions and imagination more than many more-formal works of art.

Sculpture: Tombs and Monuments

TOWARD THE END of the Middle Ages, except in England, the better sculptors tended to work inside religious buildings rather than on decorating the outside. Their work was more private, carried out for an individual or a family rather than an institution like a monastery. Much of their finest work was reserved for elaborate tombs.

France's Saint Louis (King Louis IX, reigned 1226–1270) was partly responsible for the fashion in splendid tombs. He was one of the first to decide that all important members of his family deserved to be remembered with eye-catching, grand memorials.

Before long, royalty and nobility all over the Continent were following Louis's example. The development of elaborate tombs suggests that there was more money available for personal luxuries, and that churchmen were less willing to condemn such showing off.

Italian Sculpture

Italian sculpture was heavily influenced by the works of ancient Rome. This Classical influence showed itself in faces and the creation of **reliefs**. These were pictures carved in wood or stone, like those on the side of the tomb below. By the end of the Middle Ages, therefore, Italian sculpture was already in the Classical mode that was just starting to become popular elsewhere.

This is the tomb of Ines de Castoi, the mistress of King Peter I of Portugal before he became king. The monument is in the Church of Santa Anna Monastery, Alcobaça, Portugal.

Wonders of Westminster

The best surviving group of medieval tombs is in London's Westminster Abbey. Three of the oldest are of Edmund, Earl of Lancaster, his wife Aveline, and Aymer, Earl of Pembroke. Completed in the late thirteenth and early fourteenth centuries, each one is topped with a beautifully crafted **effigy** of the dead person inside.

Sadly, the finest tomb in the cathedral, that of St. Edward the Confessor (1042–1066), has twice had to be rebuilt after serious damage. It is now just a shadow of the magnificent monument first erected by King Henry III (1216–1272).

Nearby is the tomb of Eleanor of Castile (died 1290), the beloved wife of King Edward I (see above right). William Torel, a London goldsmith, adorned the queen's tomb with a beautiful bronze statue of her—the first of its kind in Britain.

This is the tomb of Eleanor of Castile in Westminster Abbey, London. Two years after it was finished, an iron screen was made to protect it from thieves and vandals.

The brass memorial to Sir Thomas Bullen, father of the second wife of England's Henry VIII, once lay over his grave in St. Peter's Church, Hever, Kent, England.

Brasses

Those who could not afford a stone tomb were sometimes remembered by a brass plate set into the floor of the church (see right). These brasses were often very beautifully designed, with images of the person or people (we sometimes find a husband and wife together) buried beneath. To avoid damage, most brasses have now been moved from their original settings.

Parish Churches

SO FAR WE HAVE concentrated on the great cathedrals, the most famous of Europe's medieval religious buildings. Although splendid, they were not used on a regular basis by ordinary people. Most men and women were far more familiar with the local church that served their individual **parish**.

The architecture of parish churches reflected the changing Anglo-Saxon, Romanesque, and Gothic styles of grander religious buildings. They ranged from tiny **chapels** to mighty **minsters**, although few of them were large enough to need such complicated devices as flying buttresses (see page 15). What is most remarkable about these churches is that there were so many of them, and that they were so large and well built compared with the other buildings of the parish.

This covered lych-gate is located at the entrance to the churchyard at the parish church of Chacewater, Cornwall, England. In medieval times this would have been a popular meeting place in the village.

The Lych-Gate

At the entrance to a medieval churchyard stood a covered lych, or corpse, gate. (*Lyche* is an ancient English word meaning body.) Usually built of wood with a thatched or tiled roof, the lych-gate was where a coffin and its bearers waited during part of the funeral service.

Memorials of Faith

The sheer number of parish churches (over five thousand in England and Wales alone) reminds us of the enormous power of the Christian faith that inspired them. So too does the cost of each building. We find it almost unbelievable that people living in huts of wood and thatch should construct a sound and beautiful church instead of improving their own homes. In most parishes the church is the only medieval building still standing. Indeed, in some cases, such as Blean in Kent, the church remains alone in the fields because the village it once served moved away.

As well as a place of worship looked after by the parish priest, the church and its surrounding yard were a meeting place and a refuge in times of danger. The interior of the church was a place of education, the paintings on its walls giving scripture lessons to those who could not read. Nowhere are these better preserved than in many of Denmark's beautiful little whitewashed parish churches. Births, deaths, and marriages were solemnly recognized and recorded beneath the familiar, awesome pictures. High above beat the pulse of the medieval community —the sound of heavy bells which marked the passage of time.

Chantry Chapels

During the later Middle Ages wealthy individuals and groups, such as goldsmiths and **tanners**, liked to leave money for priests to pray for their souls after they were dead. This money—chantries—paid for the priests, and often for special chantry chapels to be built. These chapels were often beautiful and can still be seen attached to parish churches and cathedrals.

This beautifully preserved late-medieval fresco painting is located in the Church of the Three Kings, Roskilde, Denmark.

The Monastery

AS WE SAW on page 5, many of the great urban cathedrals—Gloucester in England, for example—were originally the churches of monasteries. Such monasteries (the word should include abbeys and nunneries) were the largest buildings of their day. Their architectural style was like that of other religious buildings, but their functions were much broader. They were really groups of buildings, small villages housing dozens, sometimes hundreds, of people devoted to a life of prayer and good works.

The standard monastic plan was that adopted by the **Cistercian** monks, a group founded in the twelfth century at Cîteaux in Burgundy, France. Beside the church was the **cloister**, a square with a covered walkway around the edge where monks worked and exercised. The cloister at Fontenay in Burgundy (see right) is one of the oldest surviving and a delightful example of Romanesque architecture. Off the cloister was a large **chapter house**, like a great hall, where the monastery's governing body met.

Fishponds

An unusual feature of a medieval monastery was its fishpond. The Church ruled that meat was not to be eaten on Fridays, obliging monks to eat fish on that day. As there was no refrigeration, this presented a problem for monasteries inland, as most were. It was solved by keeping stocks of live, fresh fish like carp and pike in specially built ponds.

The rare Romanesque cloister at Fontenay in Burgundy, France, was a center of calm and contemplation in a troubled world.

The ruins of the Cistercian monastery of Rievaulx, Yorkshire, England, transport the visitor back many centuries.

A Holy Village

Around the main structure was a huge complex of other buildings. There were dormitories, kitchens, infirmaries (for the sick and old), washrooms, toilets, refectories (dining halls), stables, visitors' lodgings, and a treasury for keeping safe the monastery's money and valuables.

In the larger monasteries all these buildings were built of stone, though perhaps roofed with timber and lead. They were carefully constructed and decorated, and incorporated the most up-to-date technology. Many had running water in the washrooms and toilets, something most ordinary people would not enjoy for at least another 500 years.

A complete monastery was rarely built all at the same time. A sizable one like Rievaulx in Yorkshire, England (see above), which at its height housed 140 monks and 500 lay brothers (workers who were not monks), was constructed between the mid–twelfth century and the early sixteenth century—a living display of Gothic glory.

The Artist Monk

Guido di Pietro, commonly known as Fra (brother) Angelico (*c.* 1400–1455), was one of many artists who pursued their careers as monks. After studying as a painter, he joined the Dominican order of monks at about the age of twenty. When his religious training was complete, he resumed his painting and produced many lively frescoes of delightful simplicity. His most famous work is in the monastery of San Marco, Florence.

Manuscript Illumination

MEDIEVAL ART was at its finest on the largest scale—the cathedral—and the very smallest scale—the manuscript. A manuscript (main = hand; script = writing) means any piece of handwritten work. As there was no printing until the mid–fifteenth century, all books, documents, and other works produced before that were handmade and manuscript.

Because they were written by hand and because only a small minority of people knew how to read them, books were precious, even mysterious objects. A short book represented at least a year's work. Books were so valuable that in some libraries they were chained to the desks on which they rested.

Until the early thirteenth century, practically all books were religious: Bibles, prayer books, and so forth. They were produced by monks. After this, lay (nonpriestly) writers and painters began producing books in their own workshops. Even so, religious works remained the finest.

A manuscript illustration shows England's Henry I (1100–1135) and his only son, who died in a shipwreck. As a result of this tragedy the succession to Henry's crown was disputed and the kingdom was torn apart by civil war.

Book of Hours

A book of hours, popular throughout Europe from the thirteenth century onward, was a collection of prayers dedicated to the Virgin Mary. Each prayer was suitable for use at a particular hour of the day. Made for wealthy lay people by the best artists of the day, many surviving books of hours are among the most exquisite works of art from that era.

Magnificence in Miniature

There were two overlapping ways of decorating (or illuminating) a manuscript. One was to take the first letter or group of letters of a page or chapter, draw them much larger than the letters that followed, and decorate them with wonderful imaginings. Images included those of saints and biblical figures, creatures, flowers, shrubs, and trees. They were hand drawn and gloriously colored with tiny pens and brushes.

The second way to illuminate a manuscript was to fill available space with decoration or pictures. This was similar to the way a book like this is illustrated, except that with a medieval manuscript each picture was an original work of art.

As with other medieval art, the style of illumination differed from country to country and from century to century. Like larger picture painting, it gradually became more realistic. It also became more complicated so that the pictures and decoration sometimes took up more space on the page than the words themselves.

In this fifteenth-century manuscript illustration, Jesus, Mary, and Joseph are fleeing into Egypt to escape the wrath of King Herod. Mary's importance is clear from the color of her dress. Blue was an expensive color to produce so it was usually reserved for royalty.

A Bible owned by the Duke of Berry in the late fourteenth century was:

… in French, written in gothic book script, richly illuminated at the beginning, decorated with four gold clasps, two with two light-coloured rubies and the other two with sapphires, each with two pearls, enamelled with the arms of the [king of] France.

Teresa G. Frisch, *Gothic Art 1140–c. 1450: Sources and Documents*

Early Castles: Motte and Bailey

MAINTAINING LAW AND ORDER was a constant problem in medieval times. There were no police forces, law courts might be ignored by the rich and powerful, and most men were permanently armed. The barons even had small armies of **retainers** they could call upon to fight for them.

In these dangerous circumstances a secure place of refuge—a castle—was a vital asset and the style of architecture reflected this. A castle was also a powerful status symbol and a home, so castle builders had to balance comfort, impression, and strength.

Castles of the early medieval period were very simple, consisting of a mound of raised earth (the **motte**) with a wooden or stone tower (the **keep**) on top. Sometimes, as at Duffus in Scotland, the mound was not stable enough to bear the weight of a stone tower and it toppled over.

An area around the base of the mound (the **bailey**) was enclosed with a wooden fence or stone wall. This might be protected with a ditch (the moat), either dry or water filled, around the outside. The castle's weakest point was the entrance, so the stout doors of the gateway into the bailey and the keep might be protected with an iron grille (a **portcullis**) or a drawbridge that could be raised in time of danger.

This section of the Bayeux Tapestry (see pages 8–9) shows workers digging earth for the motte of an early wooden castle.

Square to Round

By the twelfth century most castles were being built in stone as attackers could set wooden ones on fire too easily. Another development was to build towers in the bailey wall, especially on either side of the gateway. This enabled defenders to shoot at attackers from the side. The shape of the towers themselves sometimes changed, too. Most early ones were solid and square, with flat walls and right-angled corners. This design was comfortable for living in, but presented attackers with an easy target. Also, a square corner was a weak point as it was not supported by the walls on either side.

This difficulty could be solved by making towers circular. Unlike a square one, a round tower has no weak corner. Walls, too, were rounded where possible, offering fewer flat surfaces for attackers to bombard. The builder had a tough decision to make, though, as rooms within rounded towers were less comfortable than square ones.

The mighty keep of Dover Castle was erected in Norman times. Overlooking Britain's main port connecting with Europe, the castle is known as the key to the country.

Murder Holes

Attackers trying to get into a castle normally concentrated on the gateway. This was defended by at least two sets of iron-studded doors or gates joined by a covered passageway. The roof of this entrance was pierced with holes—murder holes—through which defenders could shoot at attackers who managed to get through the first set of doors.

Later Castles

CASTLE BUILDING reached its height in the early fourteenth century. The entrance was now almost as large and secure as the keep itself, with a frightening array of towers, doors, portcullises, murder holes, and drawbridges. The lofty walls were splayed out at the bottom to make them more difficult to climb up and attack.

Most impressive of all, an extra ring of walls was built outside the bailey. This produced what is known as the concentric castle, consisting of a keep surrounded by two rings of walls. Beaumaris Castle on the Isle of Anglesey, Wales, built by England's Edward I (reigned 1272–1307), is a good example of such a design.

Another device to ward off attackers was **machicolation**. This involved building a platform, either in stone as part of the top of the wall or as a temporary wooden base, that projected over the foot of the wall. From this platform defenders could look directly down on attackers and drop stones, arrows, hot oil, or anything else unpleasant onto their heads.

The English-built castle at Beaumaris, Anglesey, Wales, is now a beautiful tourist attraction. For centuries, however, the Welsh hated it. They saw it as a symbol of English power over them.

Sally Ports

Attack, it is said, is the best means of defense. With this in mind, several castles (such as Warwick in England) had sally ports built into the walls. These were small, often hidden doors through which the defenders could sally (venture) out to attack the defenders when they least expected it.

The brick walls of Tattershall Castle, Lincolnshire, England, marked the important transition between the castle as a stronghold and as a magnificent residence.

Fortress and Home

Although castles were always fortresses, by the thirteenth century steps were being taken to make them more comfortable as homes. The owner and his or her family had a spacious hall, a more private **solar**, and separate bedrooms. These were all warmed in winter by roaring fires in massive stone fireplaces.

Another pleasant improvement was the garderobe, a toilet built into the stonework and overhanging the outer wall. Although convenient, it also created a new point of weakness—Château Gaillard, the mighty fortress of England's King John (1199–1216), was stormed in 1204 after an advance party had crept in through the garderobe.

Finally, with the development of wall-smashing cannon in the later fourteenth century, the differences between castles and other large dwellings became blurred. A good example is Tattershall Castle in Lincolnshire, England. Built for Ralph Cromwell, steward to King Henry VI (1422–1461), it retains some features of a castle but, like the French **châteaux** (see page 38), is primarily an impressive-looking home.

The red and orange stone castle of Caerlaverock in southwest Scotland is one of the most beautiful and unusual medieval castles. It is described in this thirteenth-century poem:

It was shield-shaped, with three sides and a tower at each corner. One of these was a double tower, so high, so long, and so wide, that the gate fitted underneath it. This was strong and well made, with a drawbridge and plenty of other defences. The castle had good walls, too, and wide ditches brim-full with water.

Anonymous, *The Siege of Caerlaverock*, (translated from the original French by the author)

Manors and Halls

IN THE MANOR HOUSE lived the lord and his family, and their many servants. Here, too, the lord received his rents, administered his lands, held his manorial court, and entertained visiting dignitaries, such as a **sheriff**. The manor might also be a place of refuge when danger threatened.

The manor's many functions explain its haphazard layout. The larger ones, such as Samlesbury Hall in Lancashire, England, sheltered behind defensive moats and had a gatehouse to protect the entrance. Within the defenses were the manor house itself and a range of barns, outbuildings, and stables. These might be arranged around a courtyard, as at Stokesay Castle in Shropshire, England.

The principal room in the manor house itself was the hall, the place for formal meals, entertainment, and business. More private accommodation was in the solar quarters leading off the hall. The kitchen, cellar, and pantry were normally at the opposite end of the hall.

French Châteaux

The French word for a castle is *château*. By the late fourteenth century it was also coming to mean a fortified residence (château-fort), such as Château de Pierrefonds. During the next century, châteaux developed into luxury, castle-style country residences like Château d'Amboise. Most of these magnificent buildings remain, clustered in and around the Loire Valley.

From place of defense to home of luxury: The medieval left wing of Château d'Amboise, France, blends happily with the Renaissance wing on the right.

Wonders in Wood

Architecturally speaking, the important part of a hall was its wooden roof. As with large religious buildings (see page 15), the weight of the roof and its covering of thatch or even heavier tiles had to be carried downward onto the walls. Too much outward pressure necessitated expensive, bulky, and light-reducing buttresses.

The simplest type of wooden roof consisted of a massive beam stretching across the hall. From this beam supporting timbers (known as king posts, queen posts, or crown posts) rose to hold up the sloping timbers of the roof. But what if the hall was too wide for single crossbeams?

The most ingenious way in which medieval builders overcame this problem was the hammer-beam roof. Hammer beams, supported from the wall below, reached out into the void. They became the foundation for the rest of the roof, which now had to span a much smaller space. The result—seen at its most glorious in London's Westminster Hall (built by Hugh Herland between 1394 and 1402) —is a genuine wonder in wood.

The hammer-beam roof of the Great Hall at Edinburgh Castle, Scotland, evokes the atmosphere of the heart of medieval society.

Chimneys

The simplest way to warm a room and provide heat for cooking was to light a fire in the middle of the room and let the smoke escape through a hole in the roof. However, by the twelfth century, most large houses and castles had stone or brick fireplaces and chimneys to take the smoke away from the room. By the end of the Middle Ages the growing use of coal made fireplaces and chimneys essential. And once they were there, of course, there was a great temptation to make them a feature with an interesting design, such as a spiral.

The Houses of the Poor

NO MEDIEVAL HOUSES of the very poor remain standing. They were too flimsy and small to have survived. We have to imagine what they looked like by using the evidence of later buildings, illustrations, and archaeology. From the fifteenth century onward, however, enough homes remain for us to picture how better-off people lived.

The great majority of the population—at least 90 percent—lived on farms or in villages in the countryside and were engaged in agriculture or related crafts. They built their homes from materials found near at hand, nearly always wood for the frame and straw or reeds for the thatched roof. Even where stone was plentiful, as in the Cotswold district of England, thatch was still the preferred method of roofing.

Houses of the fairly well to do appear in the background of this scene of the apple harvest found in a fifteenth-century French manuscript.

Huts for Homes

A record from the village of Witham, England, illustrates how flimsy the huts of the poor were. When told they had to live elsewhere, the peasants, "moved their houses elsewhere, to live in them again." *House* was perhaps a kind term for their ancient huts with rotten timbers and old, fallen-down walls.

Squalor

The huts or crofts of the very poor were sometimes dug into the ground. The walls were made of woven sticks covered with mud or clay. Inside this rectangular hovel, perhaps 7 by 23 feet, lived the family and any animals they might possess. In countries where the winters were long, dark, and cold, the squalor must have been beyond our imagination.

Even well-to-do farmers shared the same building as their livestock, although they would be separated by a wall or partition. By the fifteenth century, stone or brick buildings, fireplaces, chimneys, and glass for the windows were becoming more usual. So too were bedrooms set apart from the central living area.

Artificial light was provided by candles or lamps. Toilet arrangements were extremely primitive by our standards. Water for cooking and washing had to be brought into the house by bucket from a well, river, or stream. The lavatory was either a screened hole in the ground outside the house, or, if inside, a bucket or barrel placed in the cellar. Toilet paper was unknown.

The Luttrell Psalter

Made by many artists for Sir Richard Luttrell of Lincolnshire, England, and dating from about 1345, the world-famous Luttrell Psalter is a manuscript collection of psalms and prayers. Apart from its beauty, it is of immense value to historians. The text is illustrated with delightful scenes—some real, some fanciful—of everyday life in medieval England.

Town Architecture

THE COMMON ARCHITECTURAL FEATURES of most medieval European towns were the narrowness of the streets; the presence of a few grand buildings such as churches, town

halls, and palaces; plentiful gardens; and spaces kept open for markets and fairs. Surrounding defensive walls were quite usual on the Continent, but not in Britain.

Palaces, churches, and cathedrals were similar in style to those found elsewhere. Town and city houses, however, were different. There were two reasons for this. First, towns attracted a larger proportion of wealthier people—merchants and master craftsmen—who could afford quite luxurious homes. Urban wealth was also reflected in grand town halls, like those at Bruges (in modern-day Belgium) or Perugia (in Italy). Second, as towns became more populous, the shortage of ground space forced the construction of taller buildings, several stories high.

Bridges

Most medieval bridges were made of wood. Only important ones, such as those over the Thames in London, the Seine in Paris, and the Tiber in Rome were stone built. They rested on huge pillars that narrowed the river and caused its waters to rush wildly between them. Gateways, chapels, and other buildings were quite common on large bridges—so too were tolls that had to be paid by those wishing to cross.

Left: This is an early-fifteenth-century interpretation of how a medieval walled town looked. In most cases the buildings were much more widely spaced, with gardens and even fields between them.

Below: The construction of a major building in stone was sufficiently important for it to be recorded in this fifteenth-century illustration.

Narrow and Wide Streets

A typical late-medieval town house, still standing in many parts of Europe, was built on a wooden frame and was two or three stories tall. The space between the timbers was filled with brick or, more usually, lath (thin strips of wood) and plaster. The roofs were normally thatched, although tiles were not uncommon in areas where clay was plentiful.

It was normal to have a cellar below the street level for storage. It often housed the toilet barrel, too. The ground floor held the main door, square or rectangular windows, securely barred (and rarely with glass), and perhaps a shop opening to display goods for sale. This was closed at night with wooden shutters. Workshops were commonly found at the back of a shop.

The upper floors, usually with smaller windows, were frequently built out above each other, making the house look top-heavy. Arranged to get the maximum possible floor space, it made the streets below even darker and narrower. Nevertheless, it would be false to imagine all medieval towns as a jumble of narrow streets. Some kept the orderly grid pattern created by their Roman founders, others were planned afresh. The Piazza del Campo in Siena, Italy, is an example of careful medieval planning, as is the entire town of Winchelsea, England.

> ### Fire
> Wooden houses with thatched roofs made fire a constant peril in medieval towns. There were no professional fire services or water pumps to extinguish a blaze. When a fire started, therefore, the best way to stop it from spreading was to tear down the neighboring houses as quickly as possible. To this end, fire hooks—long poles with huge iron hooks on one end—were kept ready to tear off the thatch.

Black and white: Little Moreton Hall, Cheshire, England, is one of the best surviving examples of European timber-framed building.

Toward the Renaissance

THE ART and architecture of the medieval period has not lost its power to amaze, inspire, amuse—and terrify. Visitors seeing the macabre *Dance of Death* painted on the walls of Nørre Alslev on the Danish island of Falster cannot fail to be struck by its power. We are awestruck by the sheer magnificence of Granada's Alhambra, and by the clean beauty of Canterbury Cathedral. We wonder, too, how workmen without modern tools and materials could have devised a home as delightful as Château d'Amboise in the valley of the Loire.

Not surprisingly, succeeding generations have tried to recapture that medieval magic. When the Victorians wanted a style for their new churches, they turned to the Gothic—the style of the Age of Faith. Countless homes built within the last two hundred years also incorporate Gothic features. The craftsman William Morris revived interest in Gothic art (see panel), and even architects designing buildings as unmedieval as railway stations used the Gothic pattern.

The Renaissance

The medieval period was not neatly divided— we cannot say precisely when it began or ended. Styles changed across Europe in different ways, and at different times. The Romanesque merged with the Gothic, and the Gothic with the later Classical, or Renaissance, style.

The term *Renaissance* was invented in the early nineteenth century to mean a rebirth of Classical knowledge and thinking that appeared to take

William Morris

Born at the beginning of the age of mass production, the poet, designer, and craftsman William Morris (1834–1896) was revolted by what he saw. He turned for inspiration to an altogether slower time, the Middle Ages, when everything was handmade. His efforts to awaken interest in medieval art, architecture, and design laid the foundations for our enthusiasm for the period.

Gothic Revival: The British Houses of Parliament, in London, England, are a fine example of the renewed interest in Gothic architecture that grew during much of the nineteenth century.

A new era has begun: This fine portrait of St. Sebastian by the Italian painter Raphael, produced in the early sixteenth century, shows how painting had changed from its medieval roots.

place from the later fourteenth century onward. Like *medieval*, the term is imprecise. For example, the purpose and techniques of painting evolved slowly: would we describe the Italian painter Giotto di Bondone (see page 12) as a late-medieval painter or an early Renaissance one? The story of architecture is similar: into which era does Florence's cathedral of Santa Maria del Fiore (see page 16) belong?

All we know for certain is that by 1550 the art and major architecture of most of Europe was very different from that two hundred years previously. The new styles were largely a reflection of an even more significant change in thinking. In simplest terms, the medieval mind saw God overlooking his world, while the Renaissance mind saw God overlooking a human world.

Chronology

Fifth century	The Roman Empire collapses.
c. 760	*Book of Kells*, Irish illuminated manuscript of the Holy Gospels, appears, in Latin.
Ninth century	First leaded windows appear.
c. 832	Illustrated *Utrecht Psalter* (book of psalms) is written at Reims (France).
c. 950	Work begins on large stone cathedral at Augsburg (Germany).
961	Work begins on wooden St. Paul's Cathedral, London, replacing one destroyed by fire.
980	Romanesque monastery church at Cluny (France) is started.
c. 1000	Romanesque style of art and architecture develops.
1015	Strasburg Cathedral (Germany) is started.
1020	Crypt of Chartres Cathedral (France) is started.
1026	Stone castle is built at Alençon (France).
1052	Westminster Abbey (London) is started.
1058	Parma Cathedral (Italy) is started.
1063	Pisa Cathedral (Italy) is started. Bell tower—which became the famous Leaning Tower of Pisa—is built in 1174.
1066	Normans invade England and introduce the Romanesque style on a large scale.
c. 1067	Work begins on Bayeux Tapestry. Rebuilding of Monte Cassino (Italy) begins.
1070	Rebuilding of Canterbury Cathedral (England) begins. Work begins on four-volume Winchester Bible.
1075	Normans begin construction of Richmond Castle, Yorkshire (England). St. James' Cathedral, Santiago de Compostella (Spain) is started.
Twelfth century	Picture windows are being made. Cistercian order of monks, remarkable builders and artists, expands across western Europe. Use of fireplaces spreads in large secular buildings.
1134–1260	Rebuilding of Chartres Cathedral (the second phase after a disastrous fire in 1194).
1136	Abbot Suger begins to rebuild his church of St. Denis.
c. 1150	Gothic style of art and architecture spreads across Europe.
1163–1235	Notre-Dame, Paris, is built.
1176	Work begins on London Bridge.
1197	Richard I of England builds Château Gaillard fortress, France.
1212–1311	Reims Cathedral (France) is built.
1220–1258	Salisbury Cathedral (England) is built.
c. 1225	High Gothic (*Rayonnant* or Decorated) style of architecture begins to appear.
1226	Saint Louis (Louis IX) comes to throne of France. He begins a new fashion for elaborate tombs.
1227	Toledo Cathedral (Spain) is started.
1240	Birth of Giovanni Cimabue, the teacher of Giotto, and one of the first Italian painters to move away from the Gothic-Byzantine style.
1241–1260	Patrons of Naumburg Cathedral (Germany) immortalized in stone statues.
1248	Cologne Cathedral (Germany) is started.
c. 1266	Italian artist Giotto, a forerunner of the Renaissance, is born.
1272	Edward I, master castle builder, comes to the English throne.
1277	Work begins on massive brick cathedral at Albi, France.
1296	Florence Cathedral (Italy) is started.
1344	St. Vitus' Cathedral, Prague (Czech Republic) is started.
c. 1350	Flamboyant style of architecture emerges. Western façade of Exeter Cathedral is finished.
1386	Milan Cathedral (Italy) is started.
1394	Work begins on Westminster Hall, London.
c. 1400	English Perpendicular architecture appears.
1402	Fine Town Hall is started in Brussels (Belgium).
1411–1426	London's Guildhall is built.
1412	Filippo Brunelleschi publishes his important *Rules of Perspective*.
1444	Birth of influential Italian artist Sandro Botticelli.
1446–1515	King's College Chapel, Cambridge (England), is built in the Perpendicular style.
1450	Printed books appear in Europe.
1460	Winchester Cathedral (England) is finished.
1500	Antwerp Cathedral (begun 1352) is finished.
1503	Final Gothic work on Canterbury Cathedral (England).

Glossary

abbey Buildings that house a religious community ruled by an abbot or abbess.

abstract Not lifelike; based on shapes and colors.

aisle A roofed area running alongside the nave of a church or cathedral.

Anglo-Saxon A period of English history. Although scholars disagree about the period of time it covers, it is often used for the years 500–1000.

antimony A silvery white element.

bailey An enclosed space around the keep of an early castle.

boss The central point of a roof or vault.

buttress A support for a wall.

Byzantium The modern city of Istanbul, which was the capital of the Eastern Roman Empire. The word was also used for the empire as a whole.

calligraphic art Art created from handwriting.

chapel A small church or part of a church.

chapter house The place where a monastery's senior monks met.

château The French word for a castle that came to mean a castle-style country house.

choir A group of singers and the place at the west end of a church, in front of the altar, where they sing.

Cistercian Following the strict way of life established by the monks of Cîteaux, France.

Classical Relating to ancient Greece and Rome.

cloister A covered walkway in a monastery.

cobalt A silver-white element.

congregation The people attending a church service.

Continent, the Europe apart from its western offshore islands, such as Britain and Ireland.

crusaders Those who went on a crusade, one of a series of medieval military expeditions launched by Christians to drive the Muslim Turks from the holy places, such as Jerusalem.

effigy A three-dimensional representation of a human body.

illumination Artistic decoration of a manuscript.

keep The central fortlike part of a castle.

lancet Tall and narrow windows shaped like lances.

laws of perspective Laws that explain how distance affects the way we see things.

machicolation A projecting parapet on a fortification for bombarding people below.

manganese A gray element that looks like iron.

Middle Ages The period in European history between the fall of the Roman Empire and the Renaissance.

minster A large church.

misericord The supporting ledge on the underside of a monastic seat.

mosaic A picture made up of many small pieces of colored glass or tile.

motte An artificial mound at the center of an early castle.

parish The people and area served by a single priest.

pilgrim Someone who makes a special journey to a religious place, usually the shrine of a saint.

portcullis A defensive gate for a doorway.

realism A movement in art that aims to make its work true to life.

relic The remains of a saint, considered very holy.

relief A shallow carving on a panel of stone or wood.

retainer Someone retained by a lord, serving him in return for food and lodging.

sheriff The official originally responsible for law and order within a shire (county).

solar The private living quarters within a large house for the lord and his family.

tanner Someone who works with leather and skins.

tracery Shaped stone bars within a large window.

triforium A high walkway in a church or cathedral where the aisle roof meets the nave.

tympanum The large rounded stone above a doorway.

vault A stone roof.

For Further Research

Robert Bartlett, *England Under the Norman and Angevin Kings, 1075–1225*. Oxford, UK: Oxford University Press, 2000.

Robert Branner, *Chartres Cathedral*. New York: W. W. Norton, 1969.

Caecilia Davis-Weyer, *Early Medieval Art 300–1150*. Englewood Cliffs, NJ: Prentice-Hall, 1971.

Teresa G. Frisch, *Gothic Art 1140–c. 1450: Sources and Documents*. Toronto: University of Toronto Press, 1987.

Index